Everspan Publishing

Fourth edition: January 2025

ISBN: 9798869232281

FIJI

By Sheeny Parvez

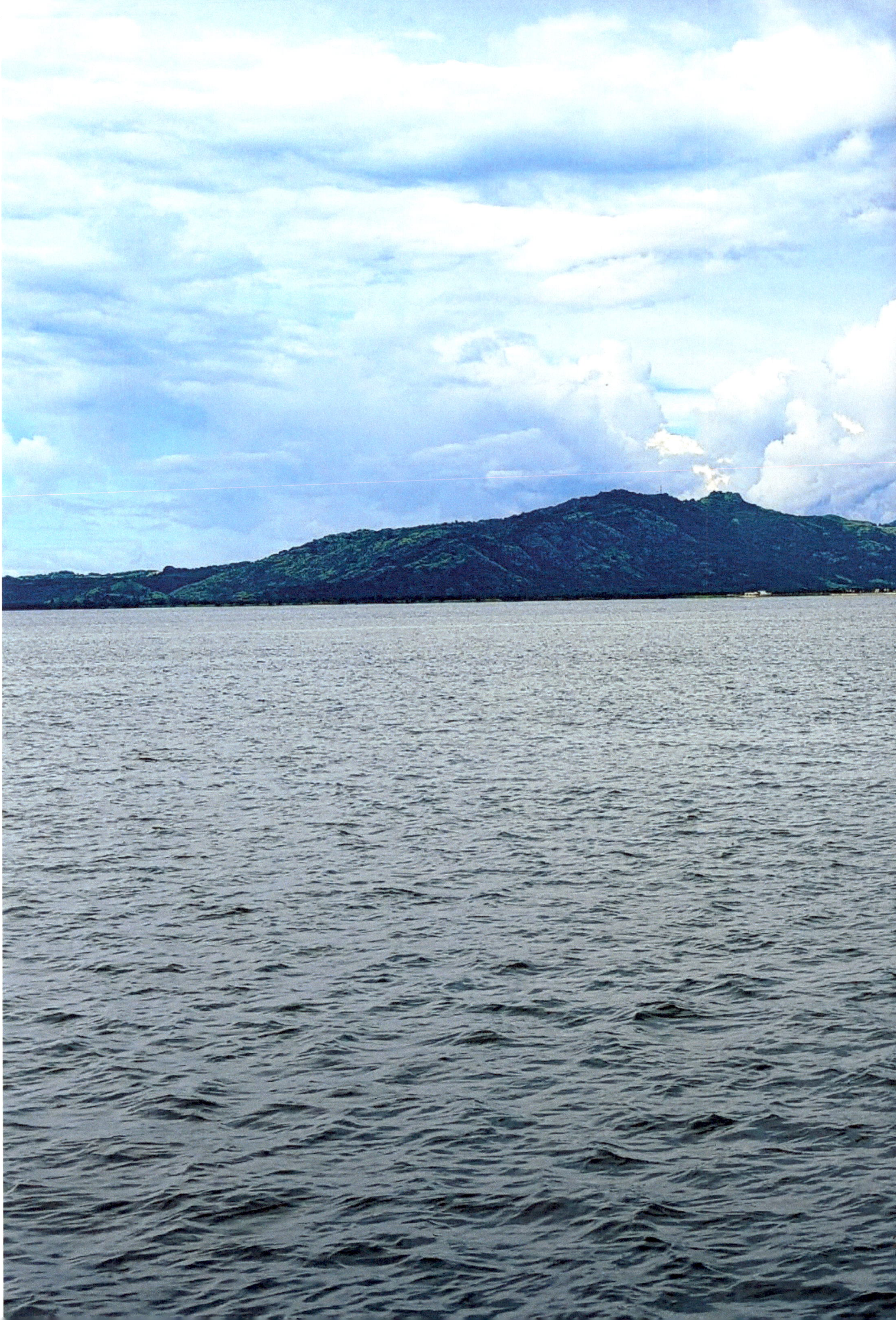

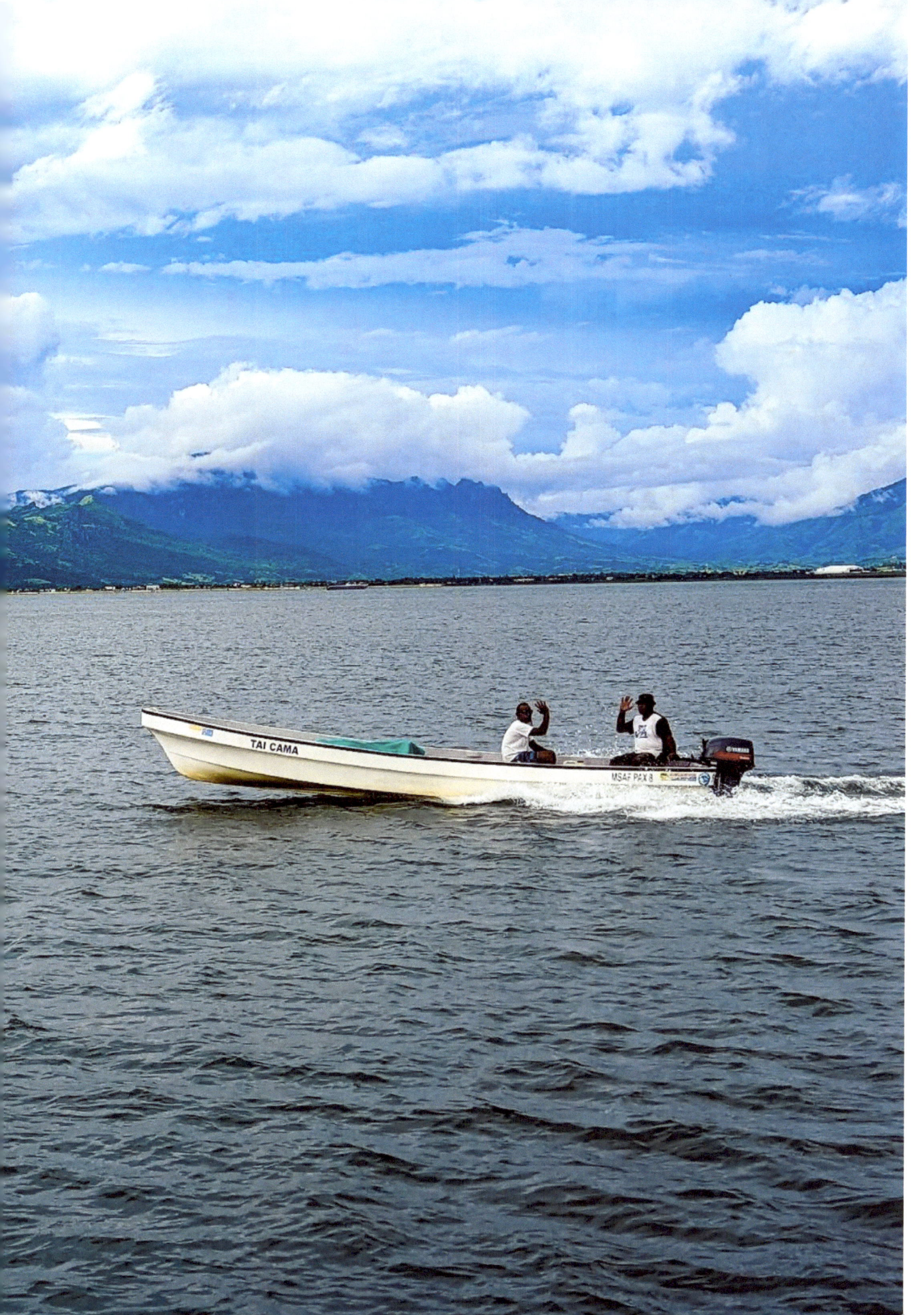

TAI CAMA
MSAF PAX 8
YAMAHA

Journey to Tivua Island

This day was like a dream. Like I fell asleep reading a Jules Verne novel type of dream. I had a couple nights at the resort in Fiji where I thought, "did that day actually happen?" More on that later, though. The cruise line slated to take a small group of us American and Australian tourists was aptly named Captain Cook Cruises. Damon said, "Isn't it time they changed that name?" It seems he's had plenty of exposure to my screaming pro-indigenous rhetoric into the void. I replied, "Yeah! Topple the statues!" But as the Fijian crew picked up our emptied tropical juice glasses, and we thanked them in English, I leaned into the early European explorer of the South Pacific feeling.

Islands lazily slid by us to the soundtrack of the crew covering the classic soft rock collection preloaded on their synthesizer. I wobbled to the front of the boat to relieve some mild seasickness that my scopolamine patch couldn't totally suppress. I took pictures in my new ("Damon, what's the word for digger person, not archipelago?") hat, which was made by an Australian company for tourists like me to purchase in Fijian dollars, to support who-knows-what economy.

Mary, a member of the crew, came to the front. She asked if I'd like her to take pictures for me. I said nah, let's take a selfie; I thought this would be the closest I'd get to authentically making friends with a local (more on that later, too). I wondered why Mary was hanging out at the front of the boat with me, until I realized - I was in her way. We'd made it to Tivua Island. I watched with the great interest of someone not expected to do any work, as Mary caught huge ropes thrown to us by a few Fijians on the dock. "G'day mate," one of these guys said to her, in a mock Australian accent. She replied jovially in the same accent. I chuckled as if I'd accomplished something by witnessing their non-service personas.

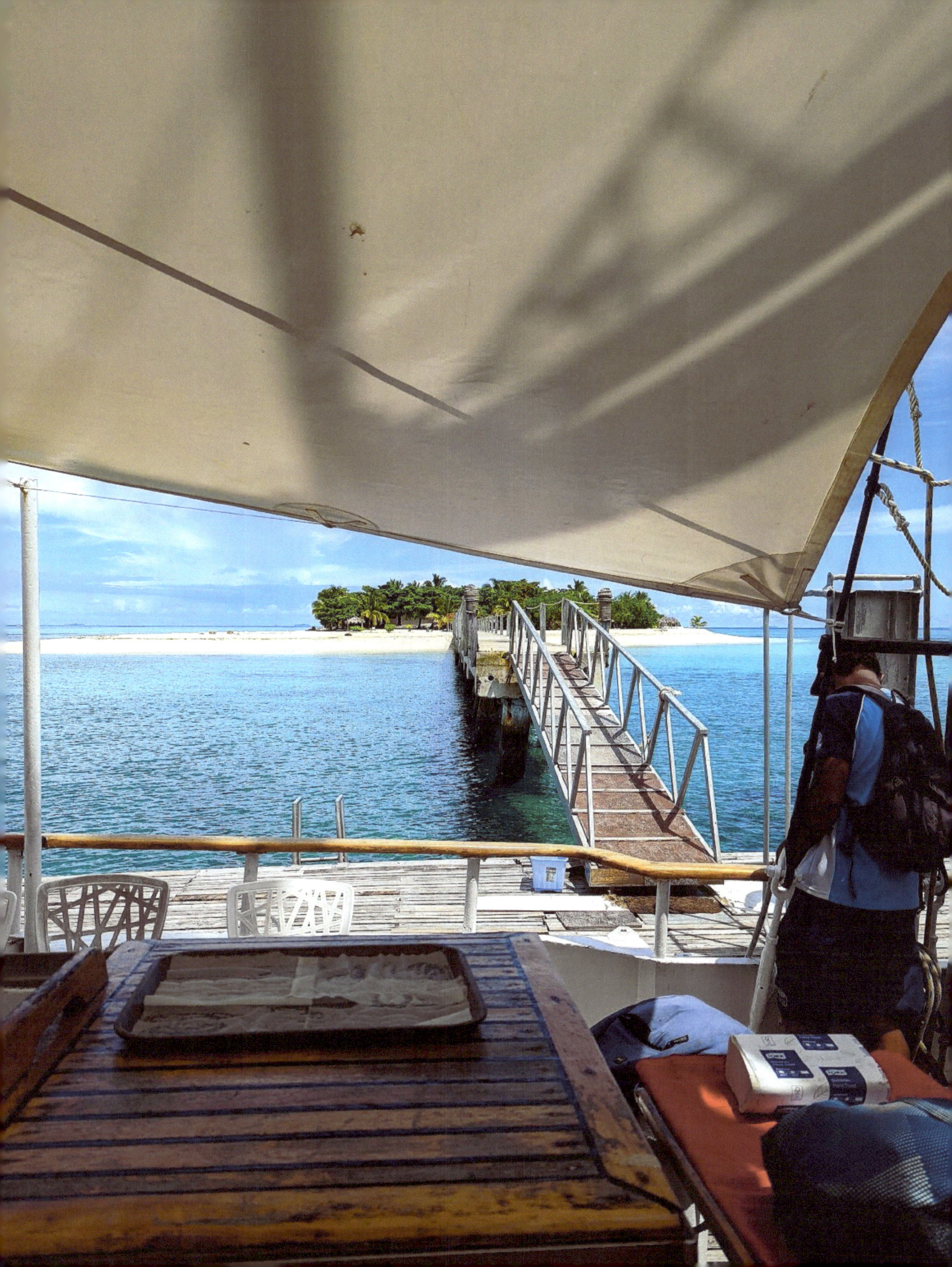

Wispy clouds, tall palm trees, plenty of sand, and aqua waters stimulated my brain in the way that only these elements can. This little island was all ours for the day. So it appeared to be a beautiful, beachy little island owned by the cruise line, specifically for tourists to visit - I could get past that. It was too gorgeous to get bogged down by the fact that the only locals there were working. I repressed my question of whether I deserved this. Did Captain Cook ever experience imposter syndrome?

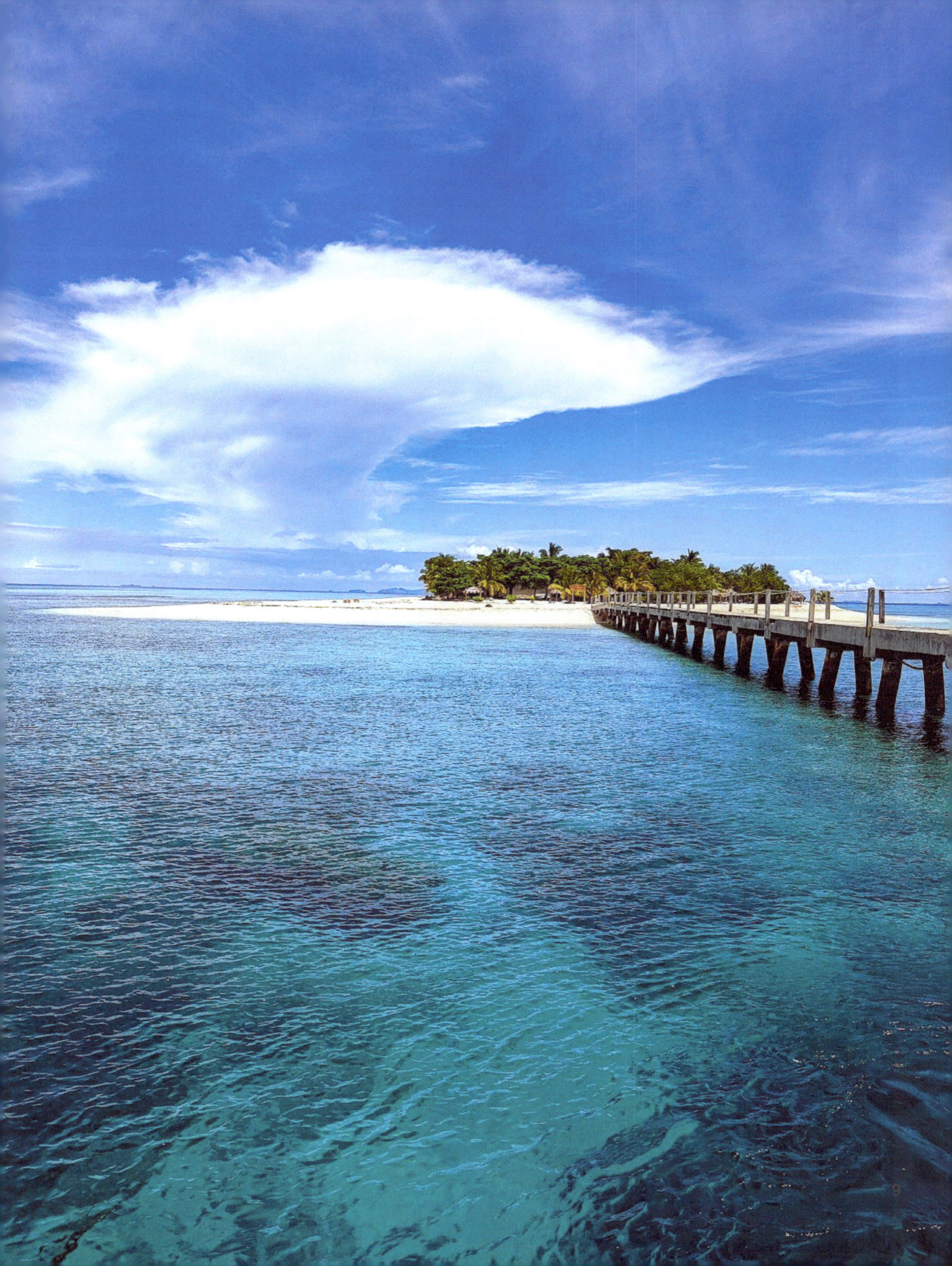

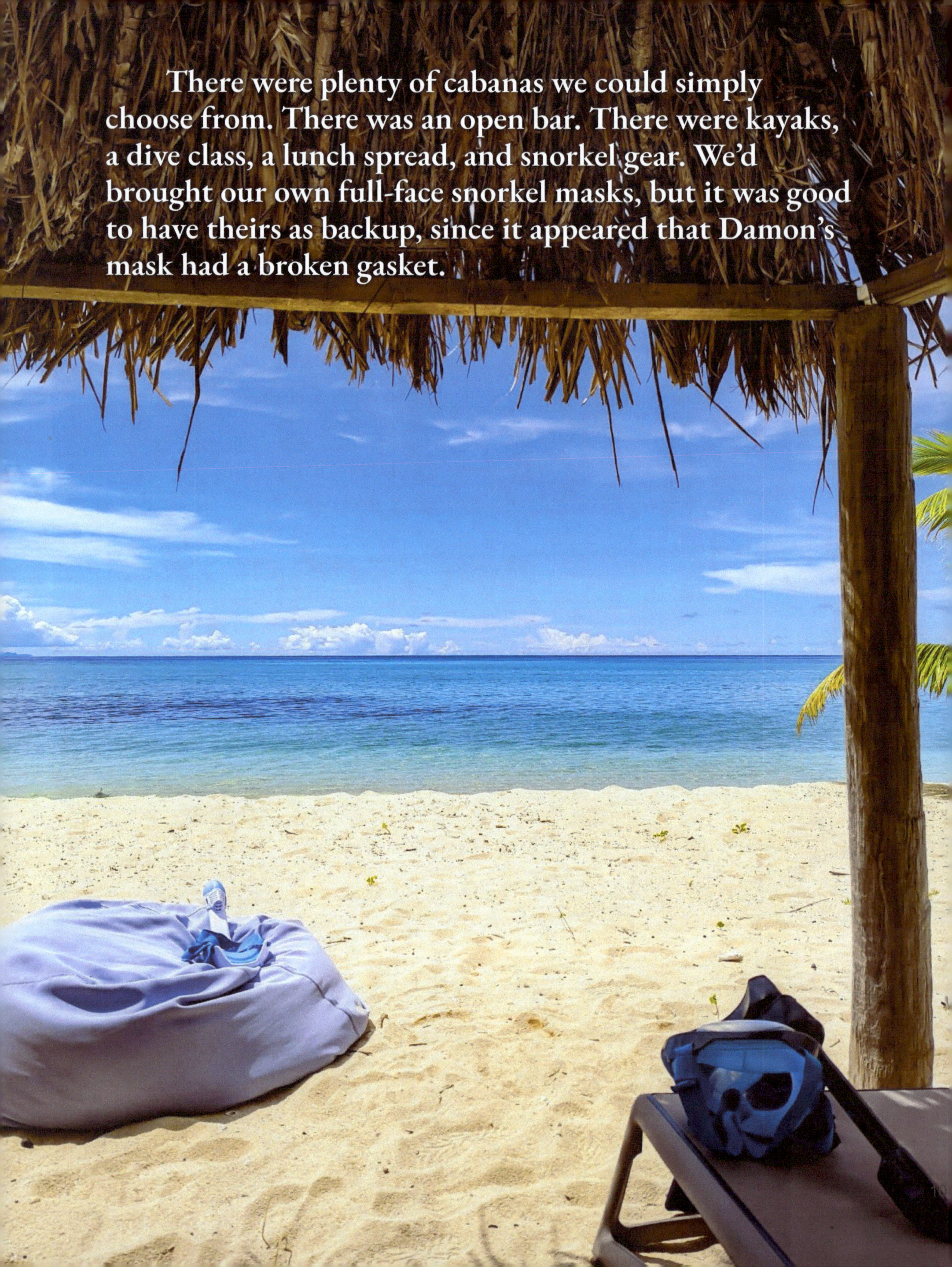

There were plenty of cabanas we could simply choose from. There was an open bar. There were kayaks, a dive class, a lunch spread, and snorkel gear. We'd brought our own full-face snorkel masks, but it was good to have theirs as backup, since it appeared that Damon's mask had a broken gasket.

We ate, drank, and met a couple from (the accents and many empty beer bottles were strong clues) New Orleans. We watched a storm brewing on the main island as we wondered how we got so lucky with perfect blue sky above us. Most notably, we snorkeled. We saw brilliant royal blue fish and the same color starfish. This reminded me of the news stories of when they came out with the new blackest black or whitest white paint; it was an unreal, bluest blue. We also saw rays, sharks, and iridescent rainbow fish. I bet I'd miss things while snorkeling if not for Damon nudging me and pointing in the water; I almost didn't see the schools of translucent swordfish skimming just under the surface because I was so busy looking down. It was magnificent. The temperature changes as we swam through the ocean made me feel alive.

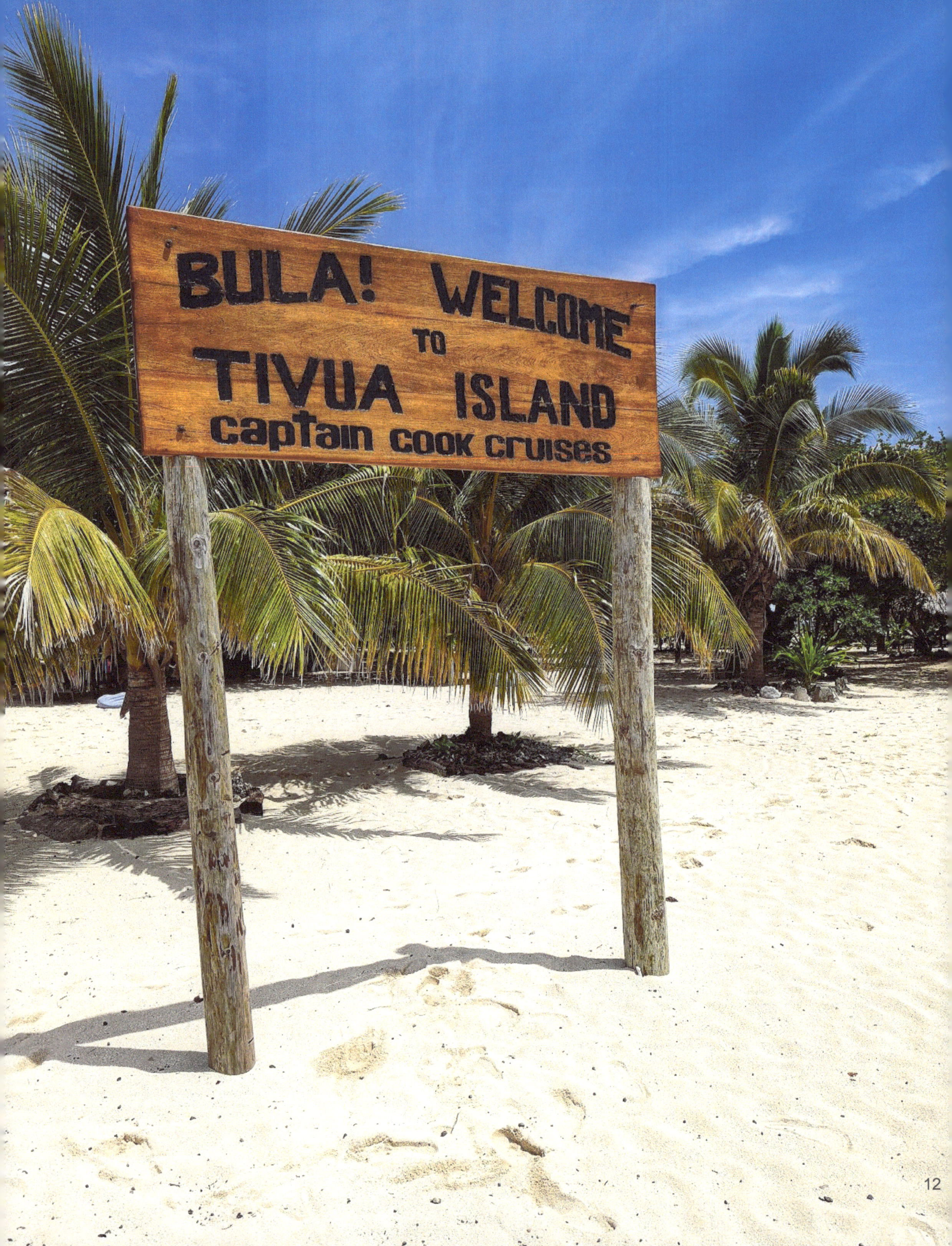

BULA! WELCOME
TO
TIVUA ISLAND
captain cook cruises

Afterwards, we swam back to the dock where we'd left a couple things. Like a kid with her toys in the tub, I wasn't ready to get out of the water, so I suggested we snorkel to the beach instead of walking back down the pier to the island. Damon agreed; we could easily carry the few things we had. So I awkwardly jumped back into the water, but I soon realized I didn't have my sunglasses in my hand, nor were they on the dock. I treaded water as I looked around for them. This must have appeared less athletic than I would've imagined, because a crewman on our nearby docked boat came to ask if I was okay. Through the crystal clear water, Damon spotted the sunglasses, which had landed way down on the seafloor.

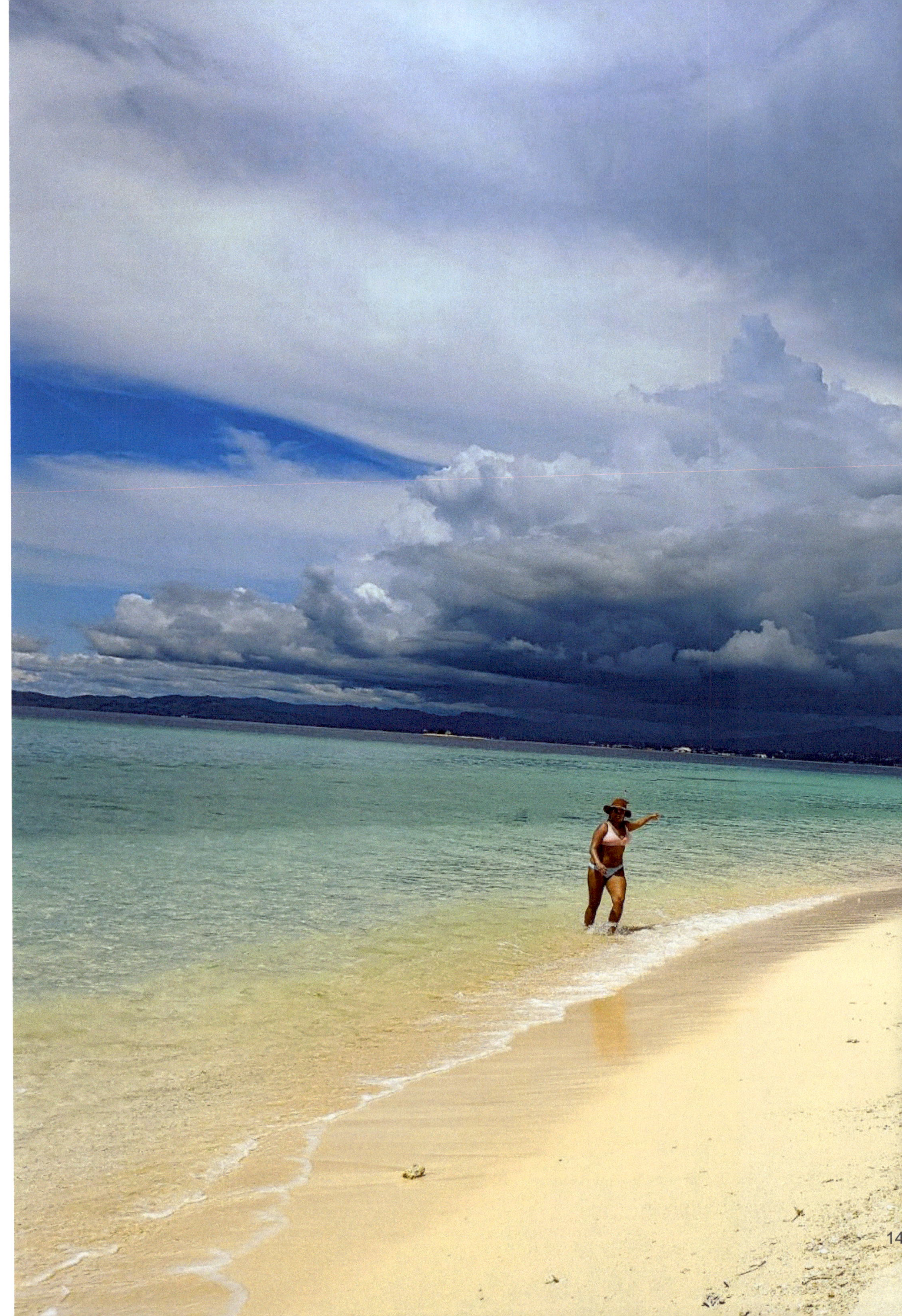

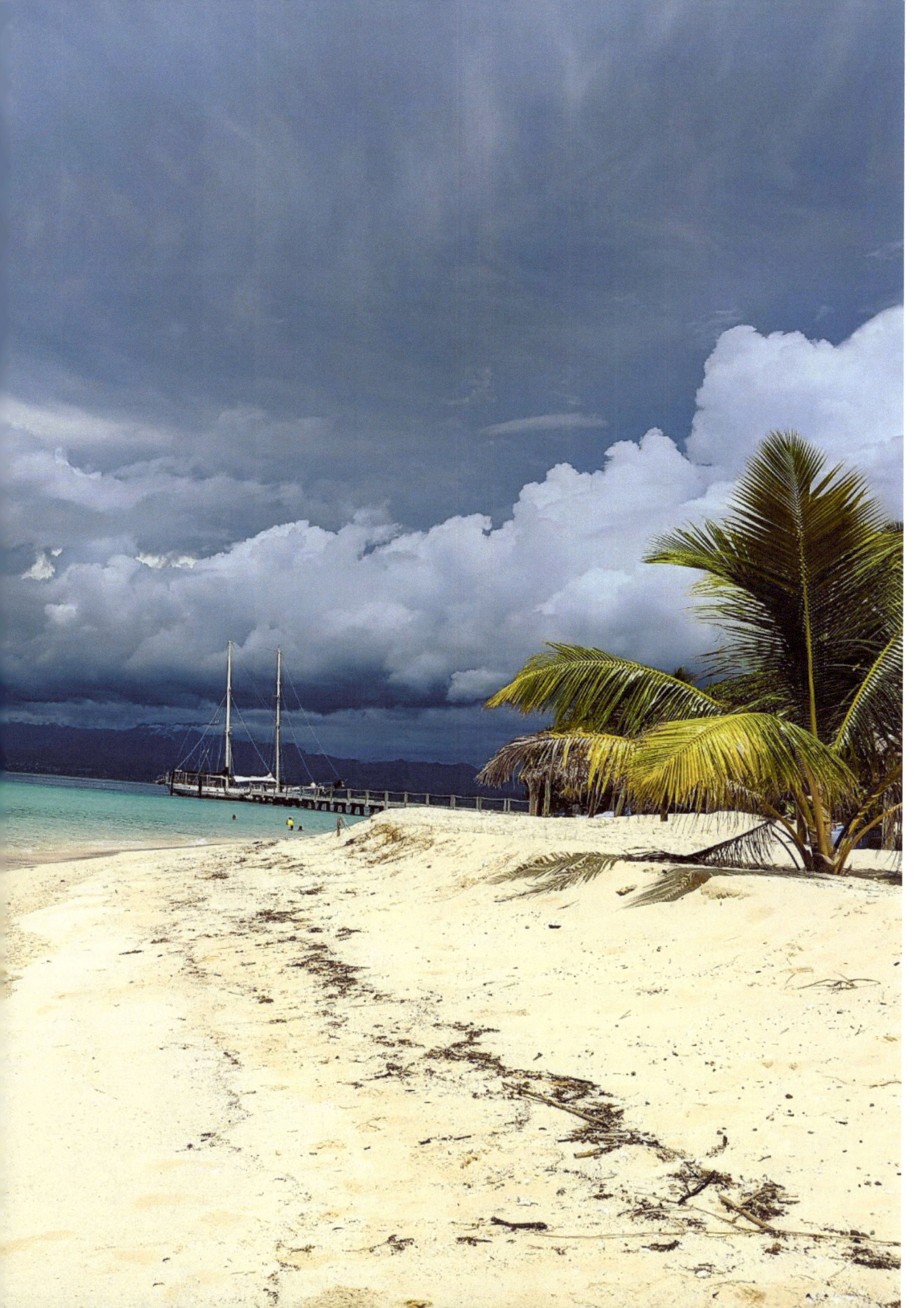

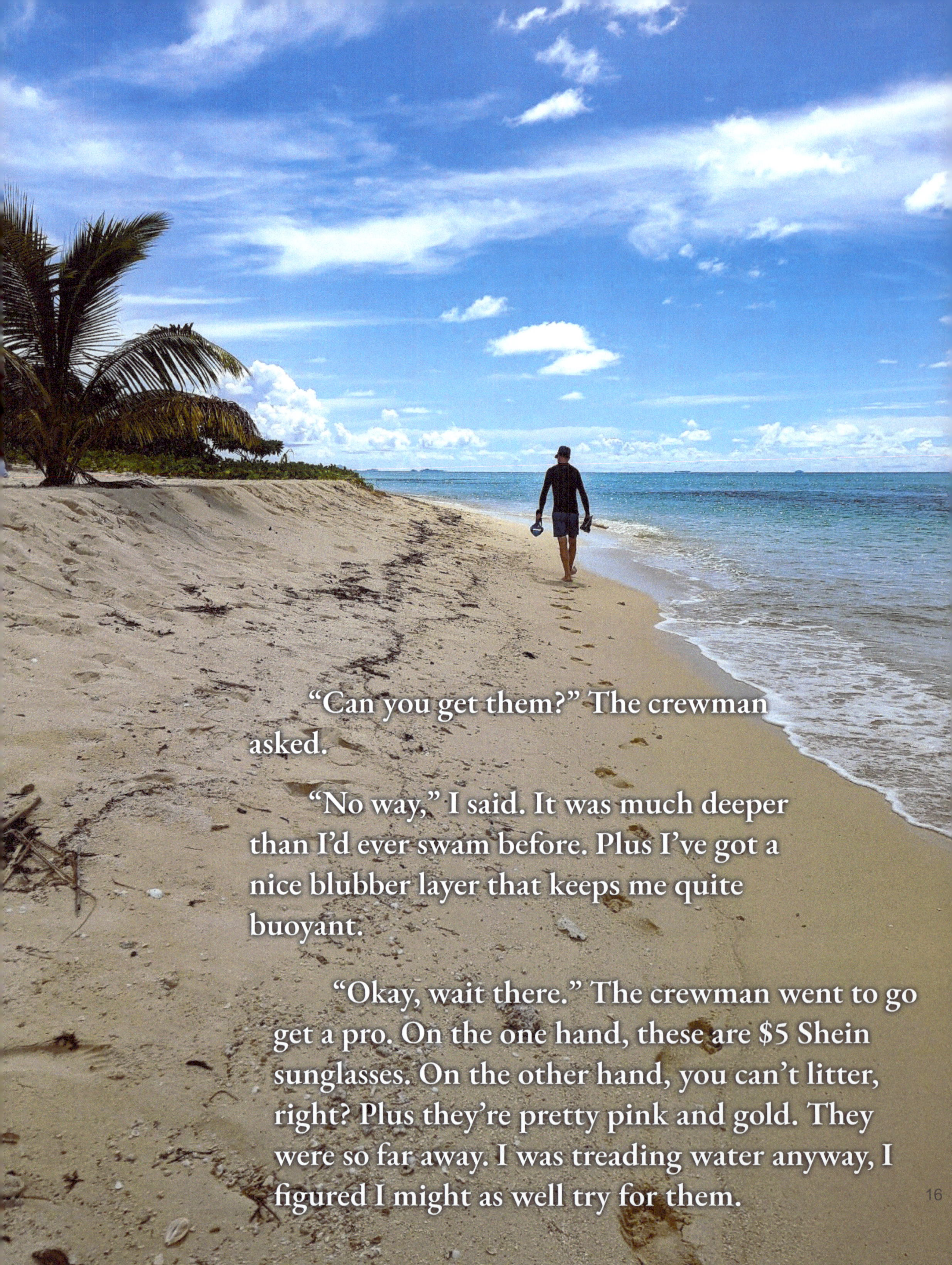

"Can you get them?" The crewman asked.

"No way," I said. It was much deeper than I'd ever swam before. Plus I've got a nice blubber layer that keeps me quite buoyant.

"Okay, wait there." The crewman went to go get a pro. On the one hand, these are $5 Shein sunglasses. On the other hand, you can't litter, right? Plus they're pretty pink and gold. They were so far away. I was treading water anyway, I figured I might as well try for them.

I switched out my full-face mask for the traditional snorkel mask Damon had borrowed, so that I could try diving. I tried to swim down. Flap! The water pushed me up. I awkwardly attempted this a couple of times before getting a good fold down into the water. I was in! I swam down. The pressure in my ears changed, weird. I kicked as fast as I could, as if the kicking would drown out any anxiety of overthinking this task. Once I got close enough, I snatched the sunglasses, then quickly turned back up. I was running out of breath. I kicked harder. I broke the surface just in time for the crewman and his appointed diver to return to see me gracelessly gasping for breath, sunglasses in hand.

Later in the day, as our boat started back to the main island, I had some extra pep in my step as I danced along to the crew's second Lionel Richie cover, while the other tourists napped off their beers. I quickly realized though that I was feeling seasick, and my patch was gone. I gobbled down some Dramamine that I'd packed as backup, realizing that I had, after all that, unintentionally littered in the ocean with the scopolamine patch.

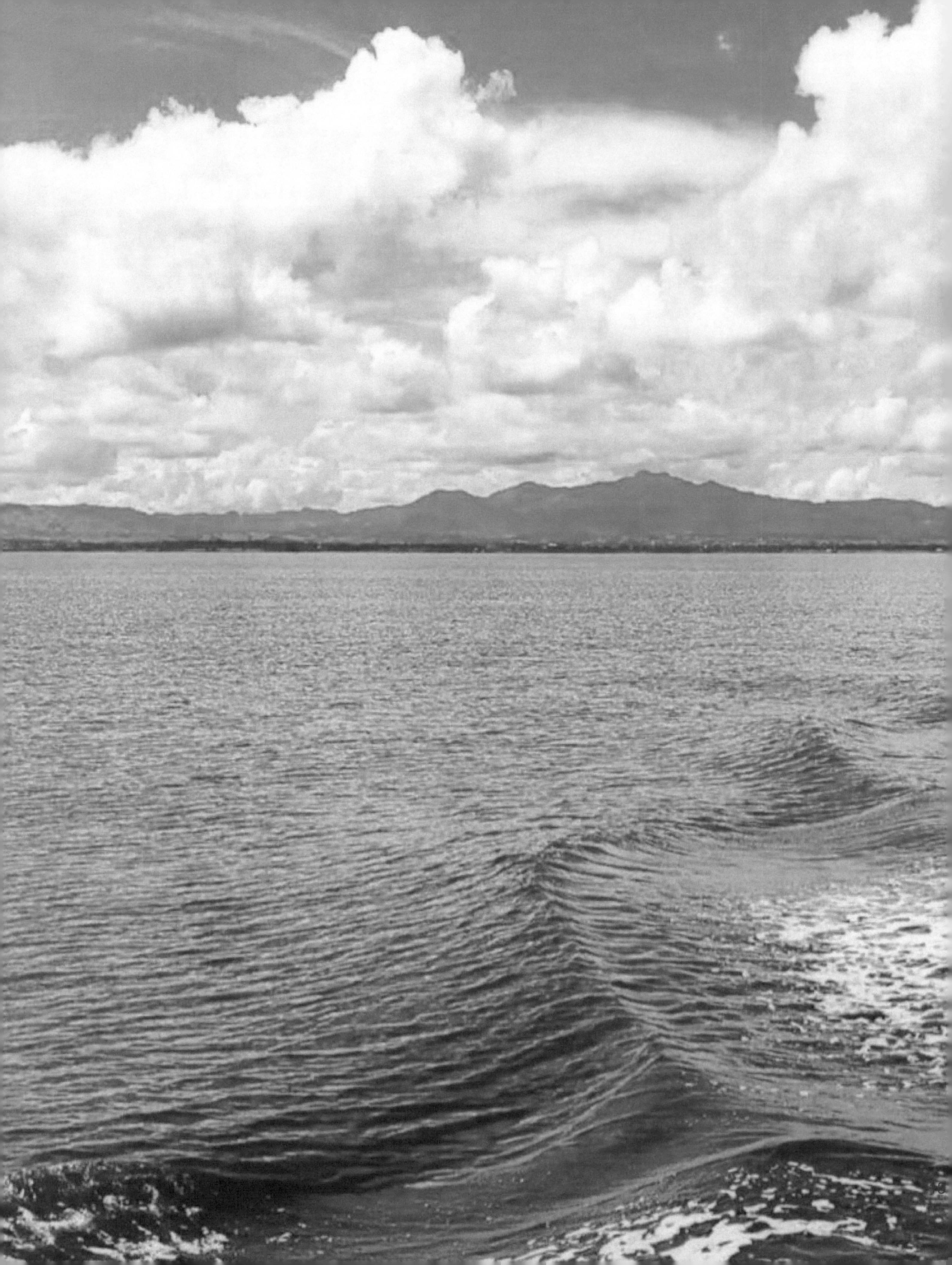

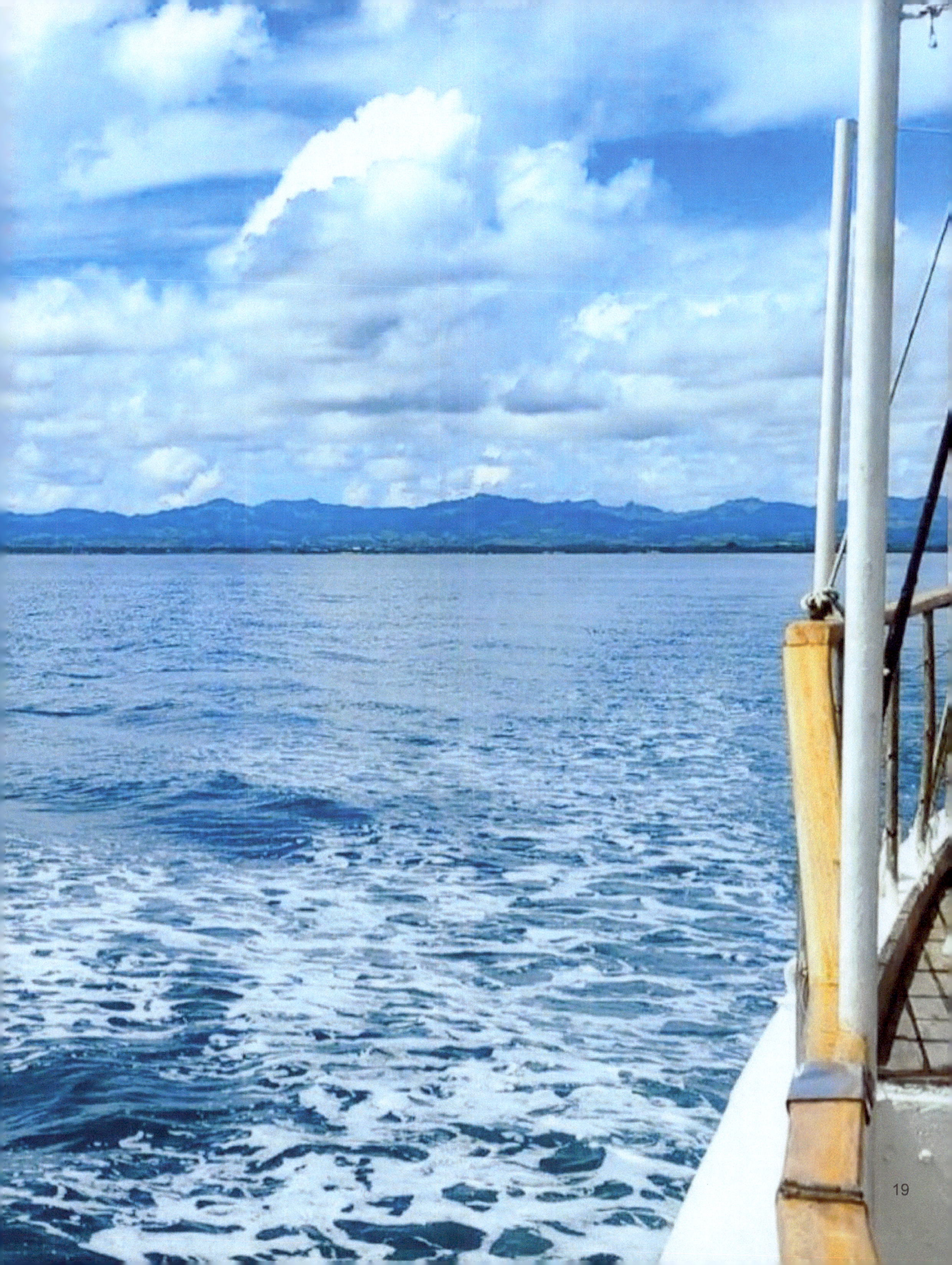

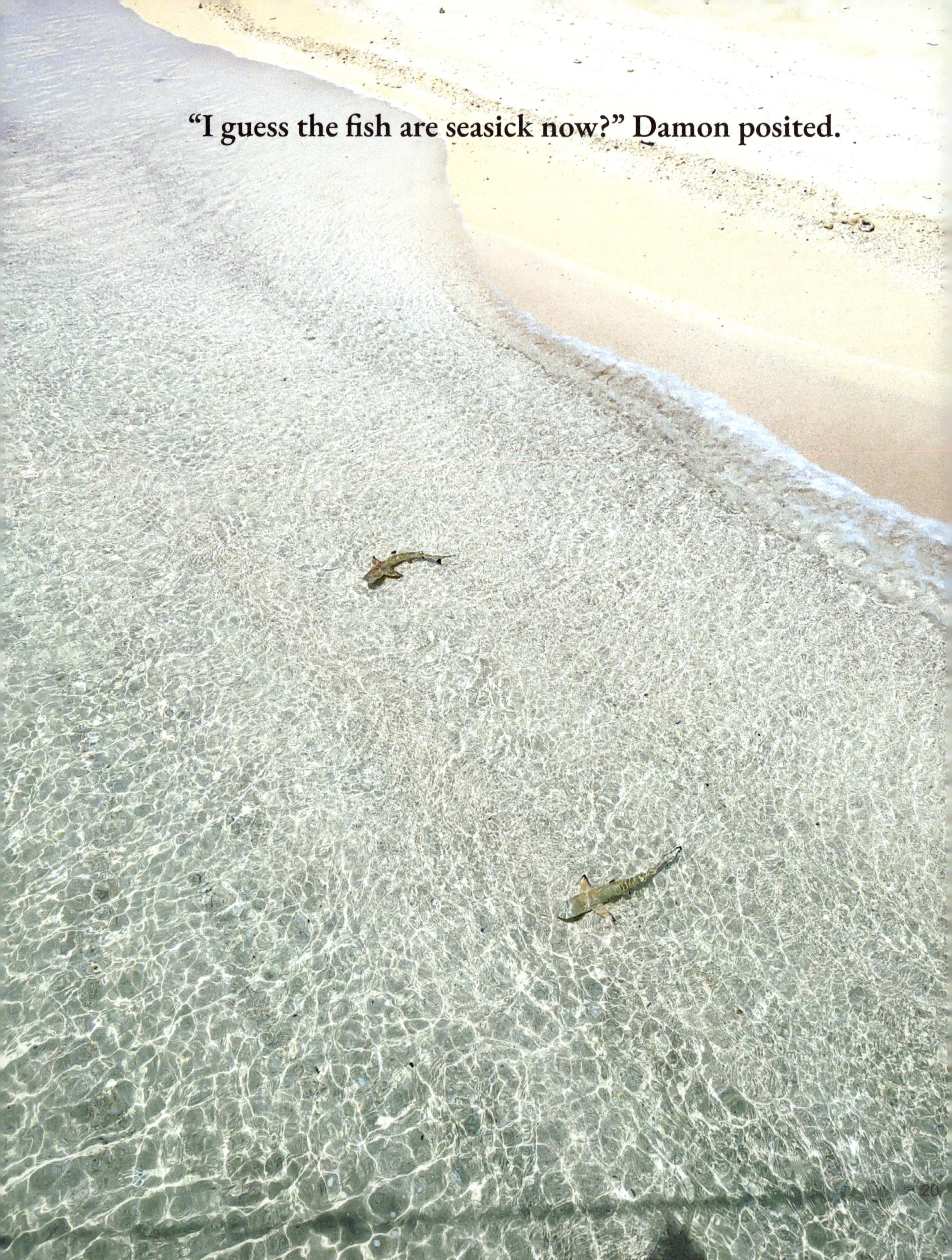

"I guess the fish are seasick now?" Damon posited.

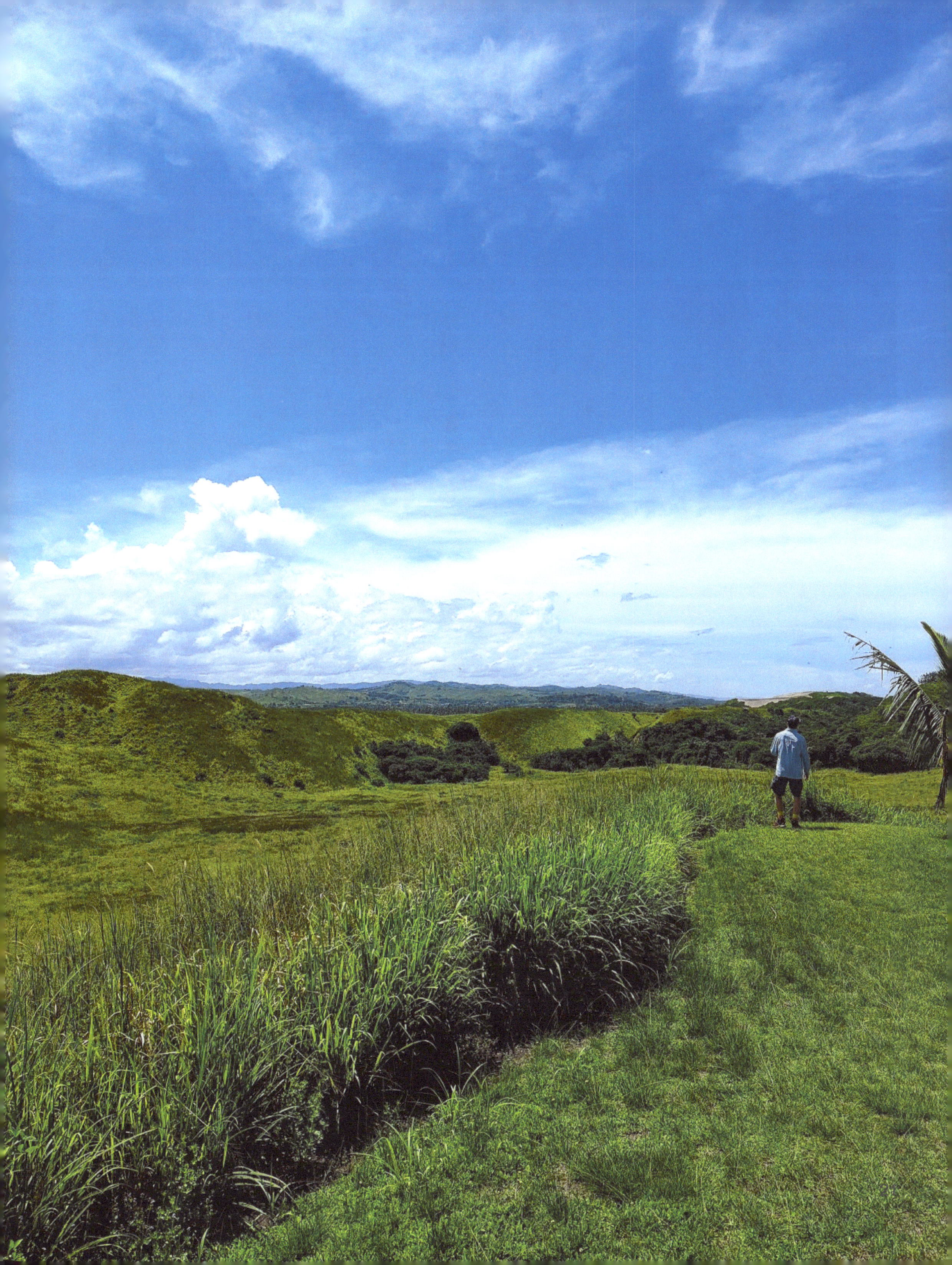

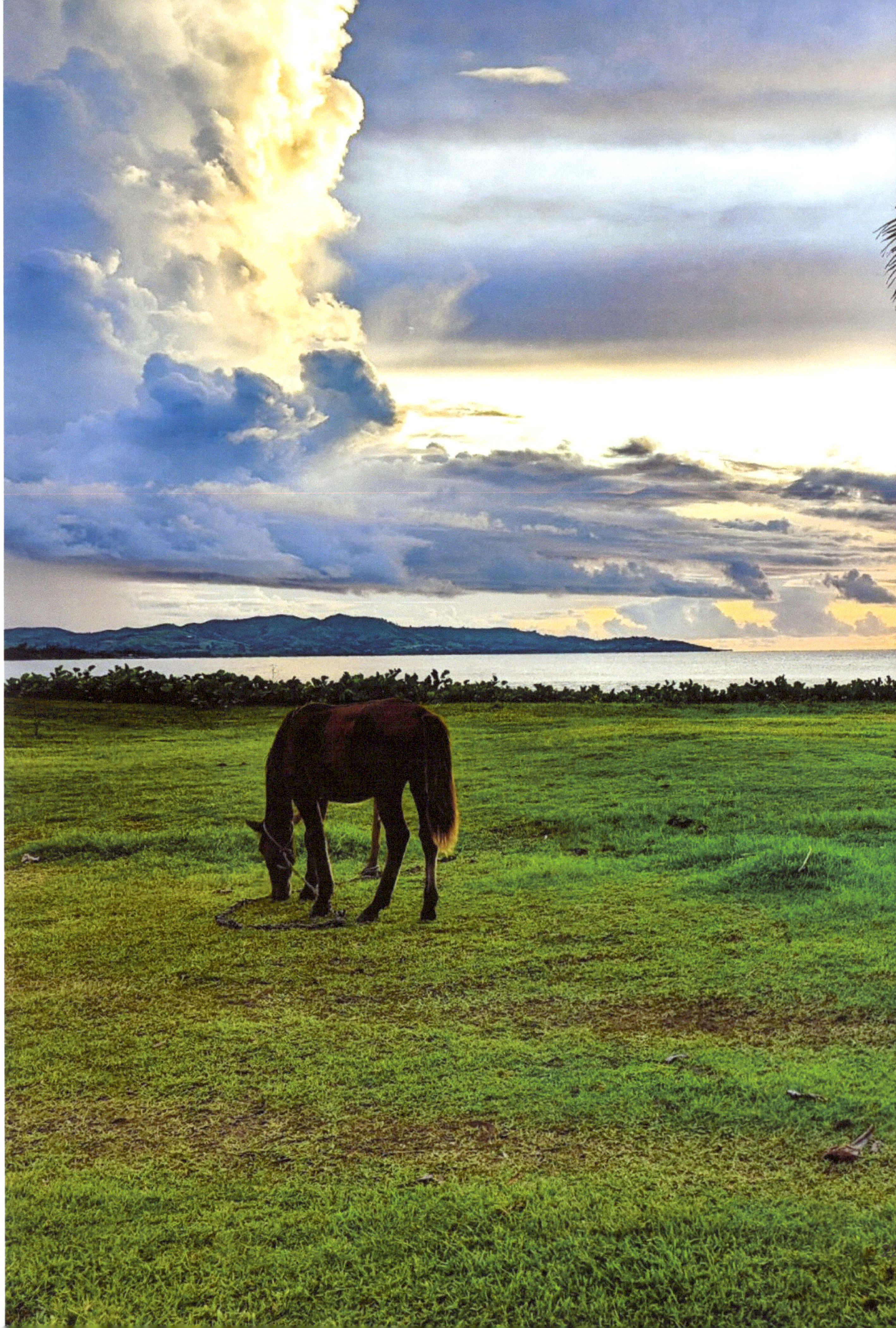

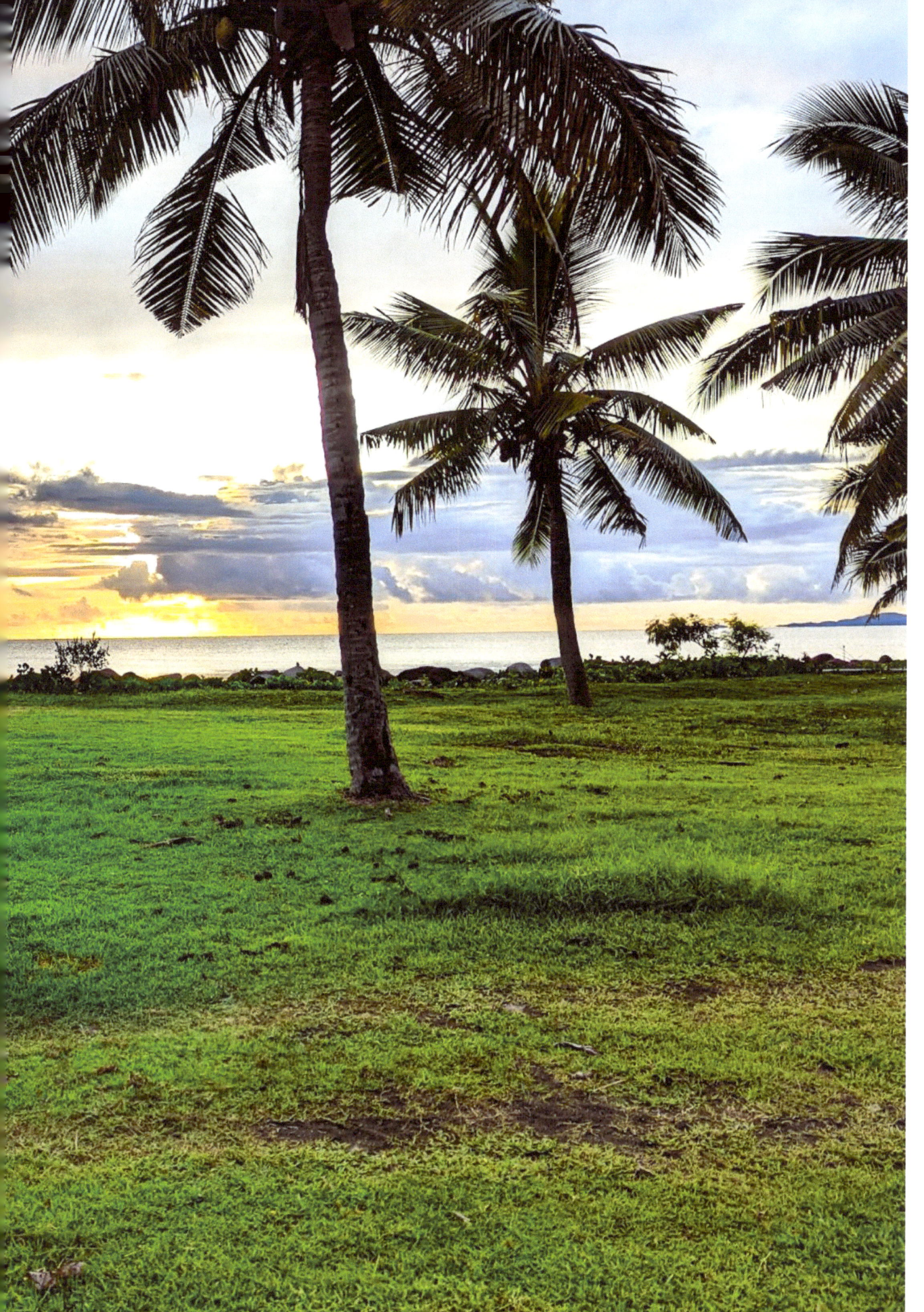

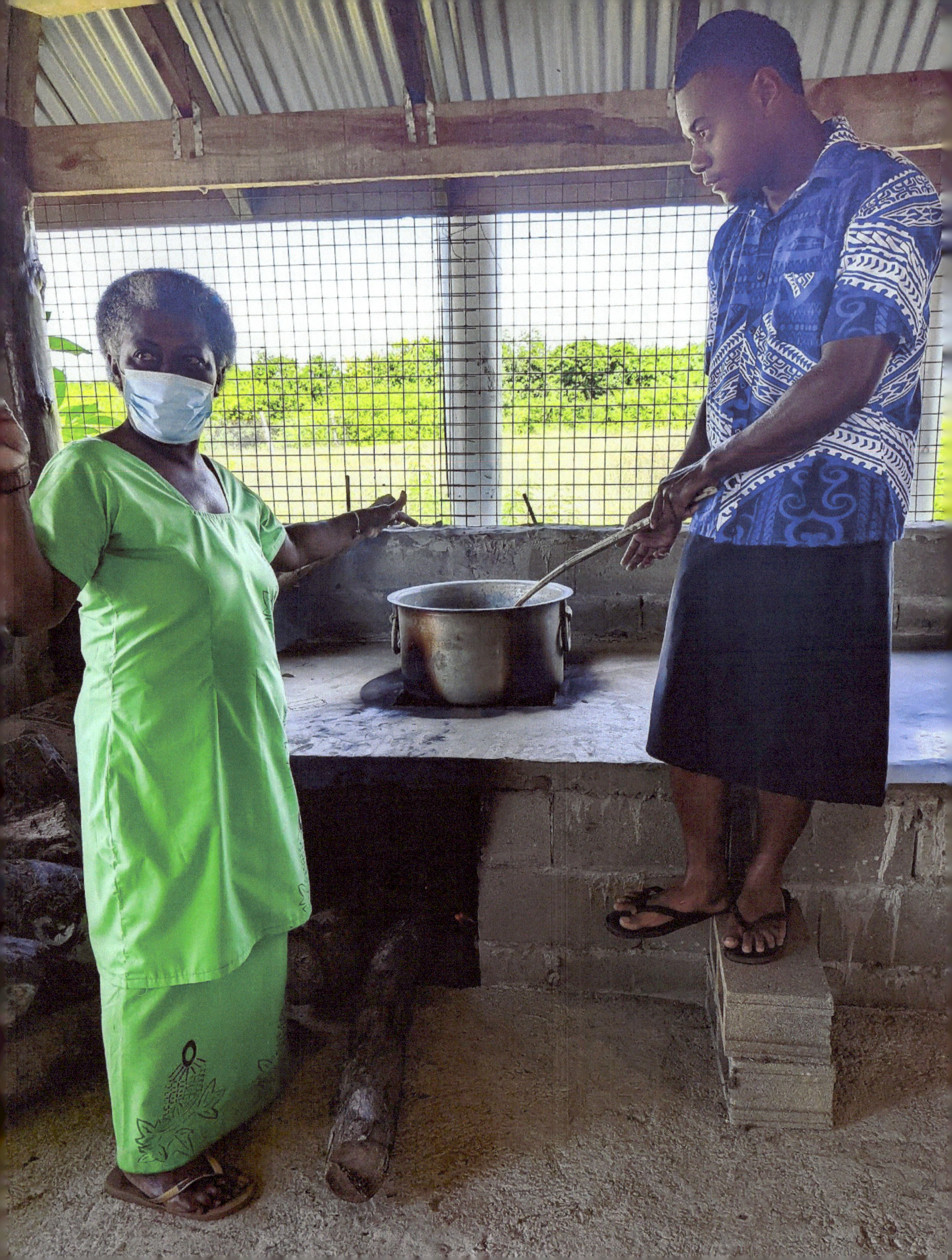

The Waterfall at Biausevu

For better or worse, this day trip to Biausevu would be the most memorable part of Fiji, with probably every emotion expressed among the members of the tour group. It's funny how the early events of the day got overshadowed, despite how interesting they were, too. We watched a traditional firewood-smoked salt making process in Lomawai, hiked in Sigatoka Sand Dunes National Park, and ate a nice veg thali lunch by the beach. Next, we were really looking forward to seeing Fiji's tallest waterfall, deep in the jungle, in the village of Biausevu.

Our bus climbed up a steep, narrow road, winding through lush, green mountains. From inside the bus, I was unsure how the driver managed to stay on course, since I hadn't been able to actually see the road in a while, but I was so grateful for the views of endless vines and banana leaves. When we arrived at the village, I changed into my swimsuit and river sandals - good choices. I stowed my dry undies and a hand towel swiped from the hotel in Damon's cargo pockets - we'd later find these to be poor choices, but they say hindsight is 20/20.

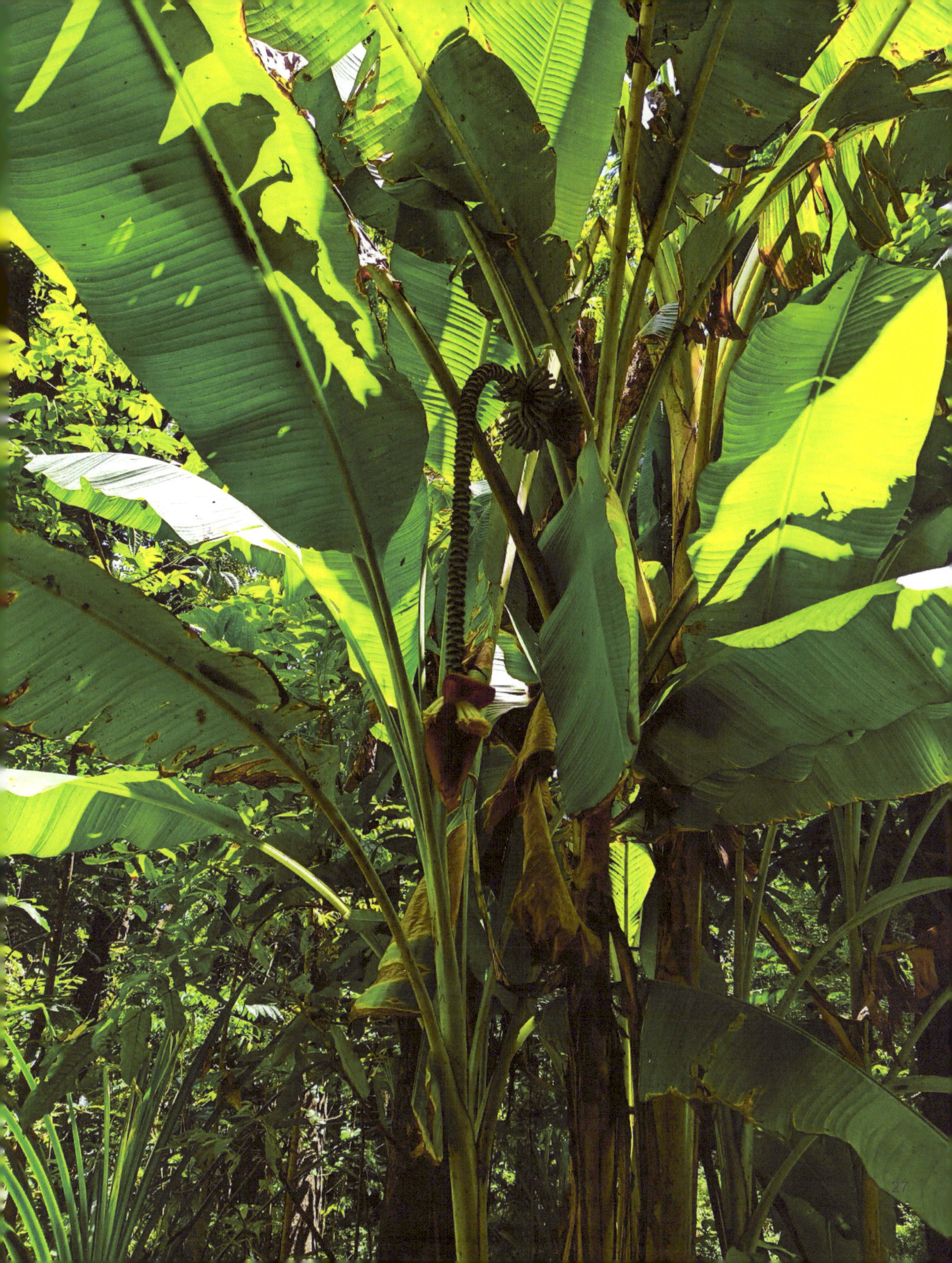

We were expecting to hike up a steady incline through the jungle, intercepting nine creek crossings. Easy, peasy. I'd done hikes uphill and across creeks numerous times, and I was energized by the blind excitement of taking a dip in this famous waterfall. I closely followed our guide, Grace, along a narrow concrete path, listening to her in awe as she pointed out various local flora, like pawpaw and noni. I wondered why she carried a first aid kit.

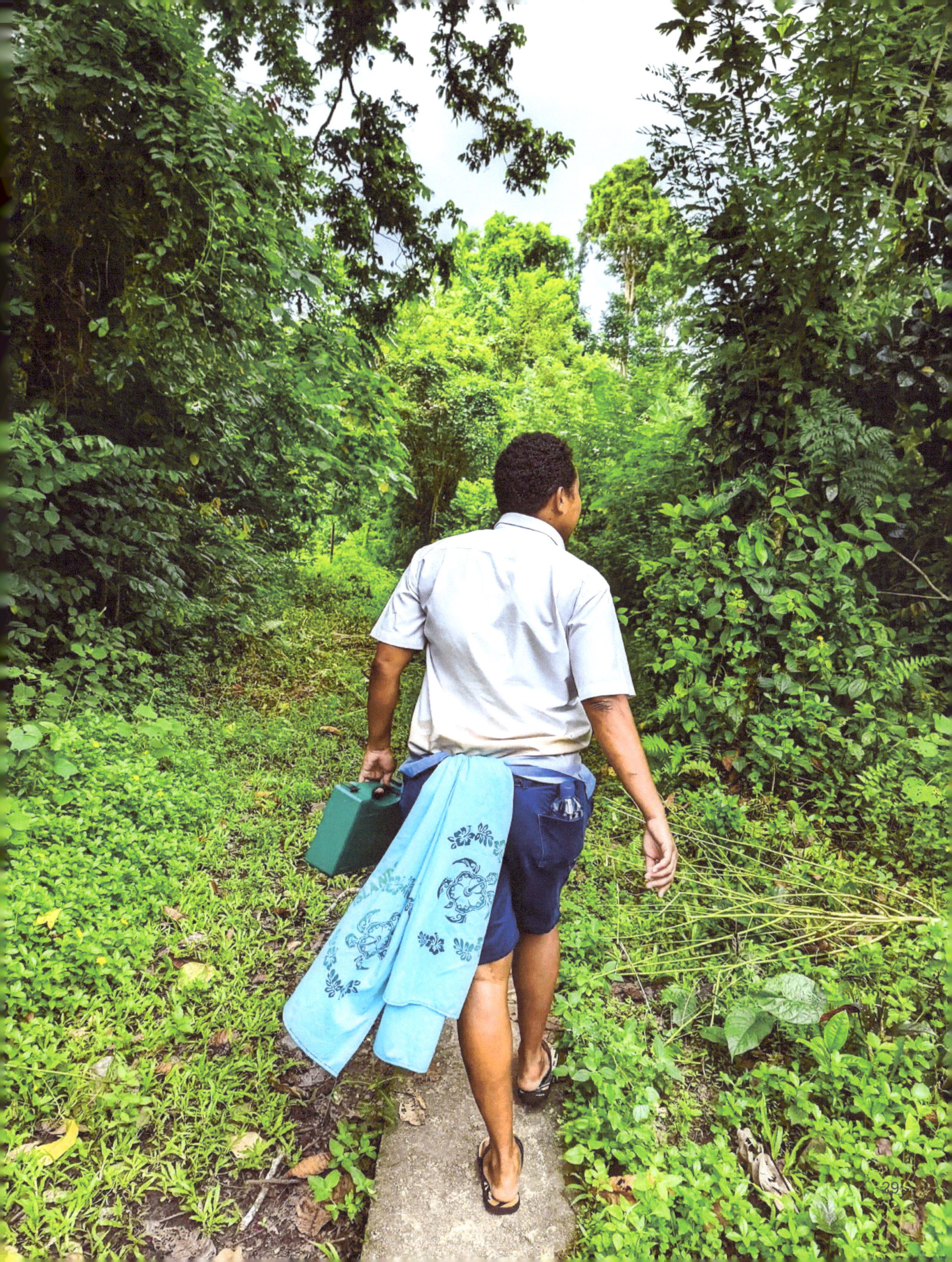

We crossed the creek four times. Fed by the waterfall, the creek was cool and clear, with rocks and pebbles paving the creekbed. Practically a Texas river fish, I was confident as ever in my well-broken-in amphibious sandals, wading through mere ankle-deep water. Damon and Grace helped some of the others cross, further boosting my ego. Then the rain started.

When it first starts to rain, there are these funny little things you do to stay as dry as possible. For example, I remember thinking, "I'm actually dry behind this face mask, so I'll keep it on," and, "it's nice that this hat is actually keeping the rain off my hair," and, "at least if my white shirt gets dirty, I can bleach it." I definitely abandoned those thoughts that day.

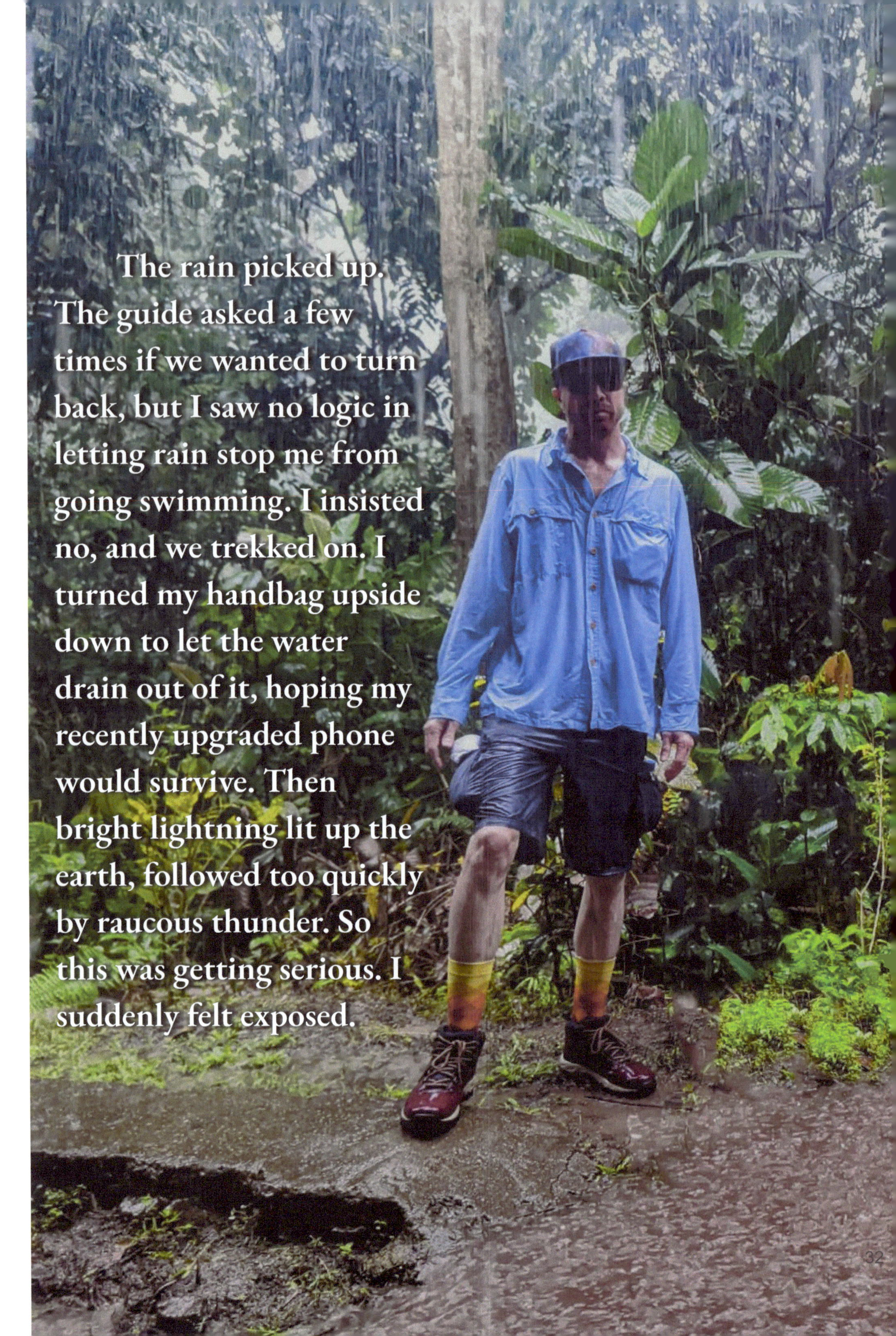

The rain picked up. The guide asked a few times if we wanted to turn back, but I saw no logic in letting rain stop me from going swimming. I insisted no, and we trekked on. I turned my handbag upside down to let the water drain out of it, hoping my recently upgraded phone would survive. Then bright lightning lit up the earth, followed too quickly by raucous thunder. So this was getting serious. I suddenly felt exposed.

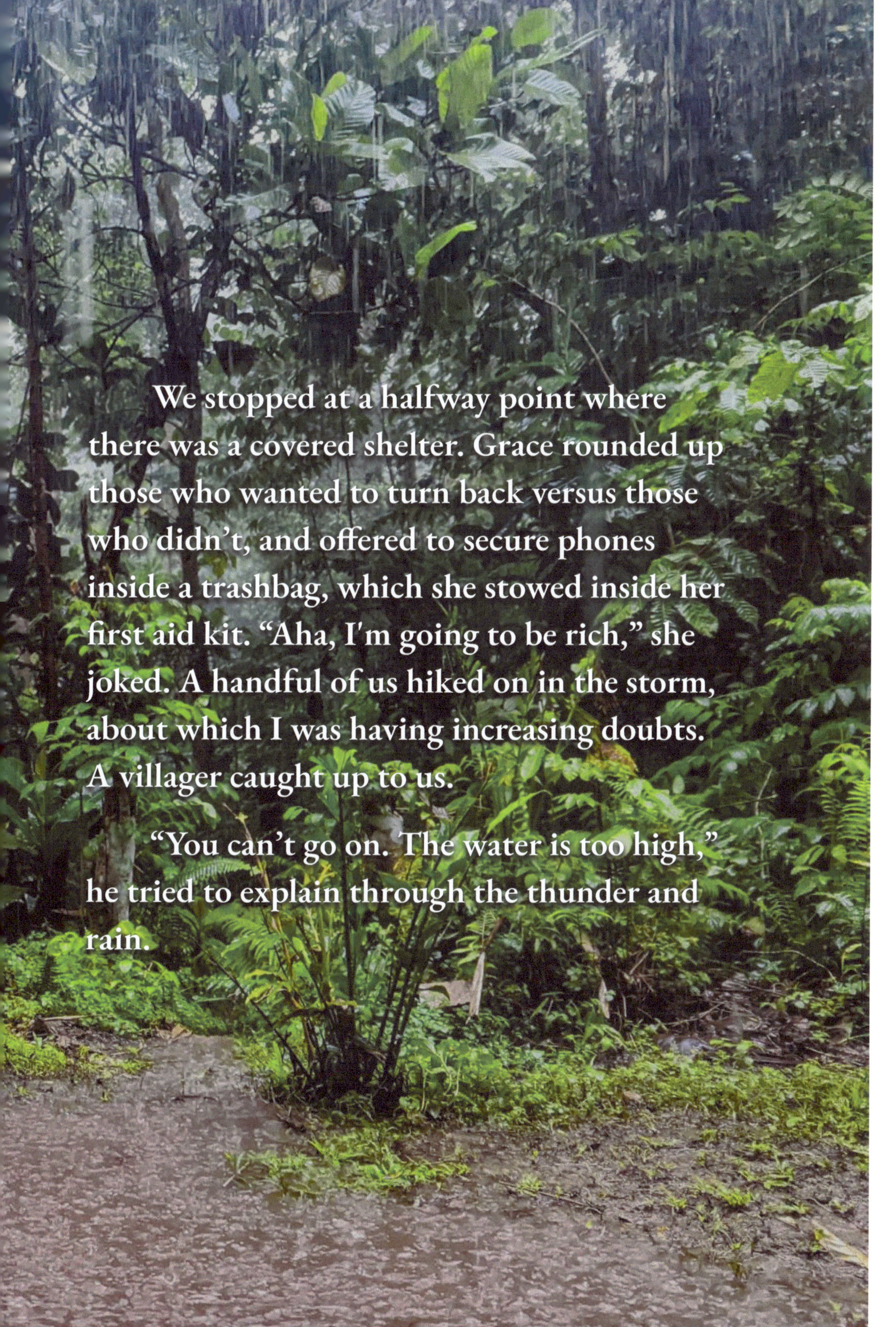

We stopped at a halfway point where there was a covered shelter. Grace rounded up those who wanted to turn back versus those who didn't, and offered to secure phones inside a trashbag, which she stowed inside her first aid kit. "Aha, I'm going to be rich," she joked. A handful of us hiked on in the storm, about which I was having increasing doubts. A villager caught up to us.

"You can't go on. The water is too high," he tried to explain through the thunder and rain.

"But I can swim," I pressed. He shook his head and led us to the next crossing so we could see what he meant. The height of the water, which now looked more like chocolate milk, was maybe chest high at this crossing. But this was not the issue. It was gushing at a speed fast enough to instantly sweep away and surely kill any tourist dumb enough to step in it. I was shocked, and had to finally accept that I was not going to see this waterfall. Unfortunately, that wasn't the only issue at hand.

The villager explained that the creek had risen on the way back, too. We'd have to wait at the midway shelter for the water level to go down. And so our entire group waited there for hours. The cold of my wet clothes started to set in. Each time the villager or Grace went down to check the water level and came back, head shaking no, I felt a bit colder. I started to worry that it would be dark soon and we wouldn't make it back. During this time, more local village guys appeared at our shelter, until there were about 20 of them.

"Don't worry," the oldest man said. "I care about your safety. We will help you get out."

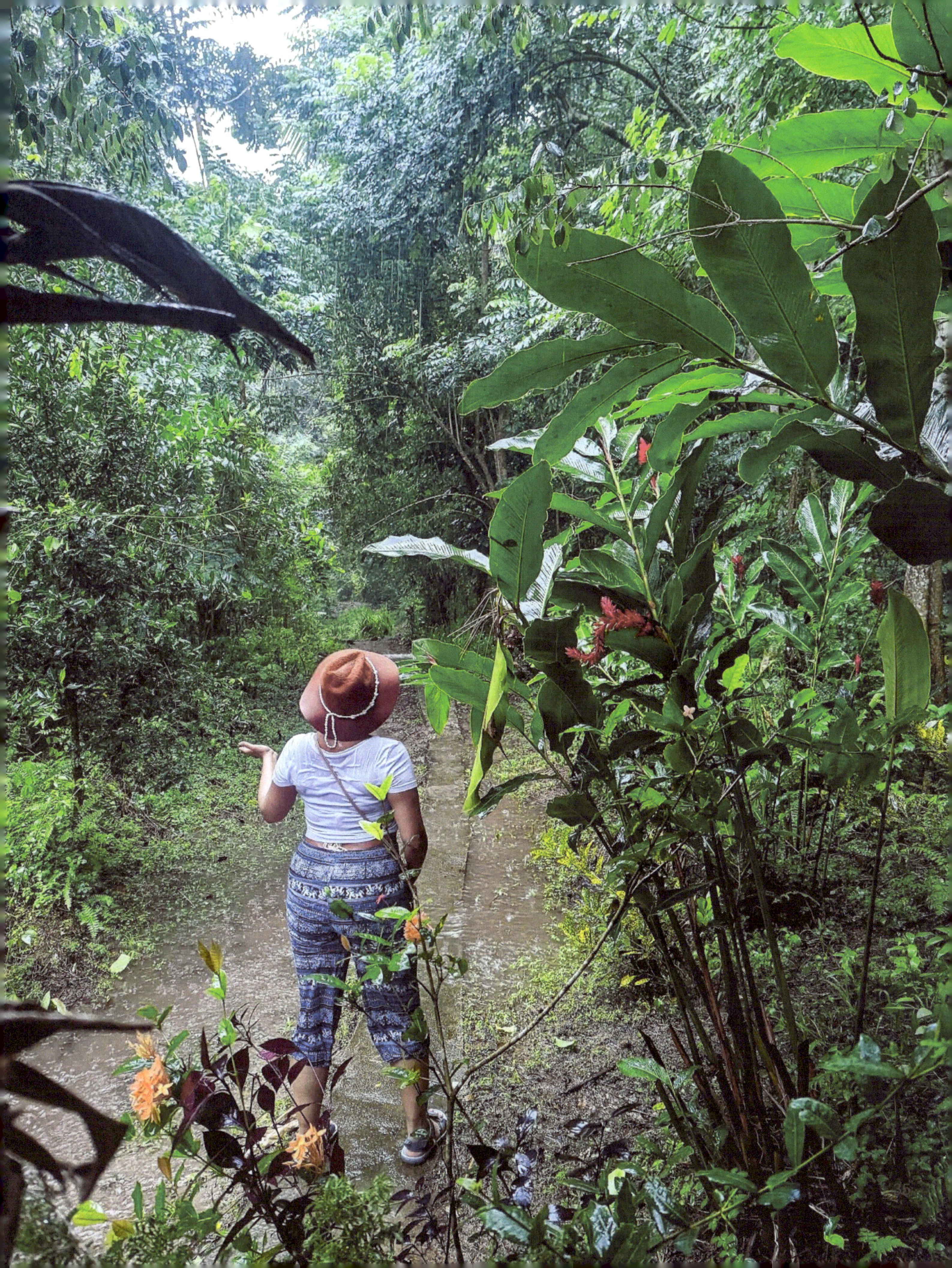

We finally got the signal that it was okay to turn back. When we arrived at the previous crossing, the villagers got in the water, forming a human chain in the now waist-high river. One at a time, we crossed cautiously, bracing ourselves against each of these men as we traversed. The far side of this crossing was dicey, as the water was flowing harder than it looked. I lost my footing, but the guys caught me and led me safely to the riverbank. A couple other women, more svelte than I, had to be carried.

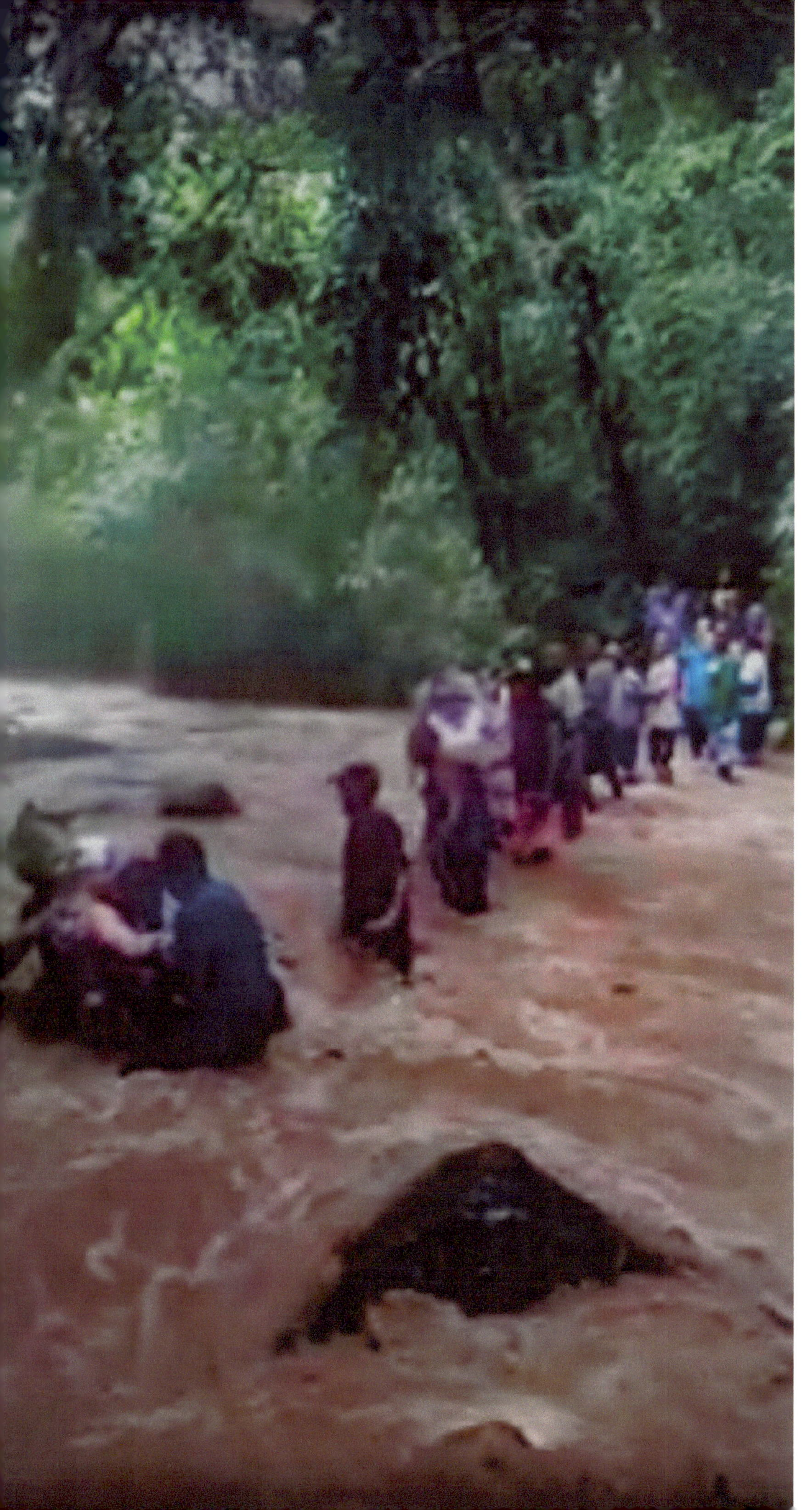

One of the guys wore my handbag around his neck until we were all safely crossed. They cared for everyone else's sunglasses and knickknacks the same way. Even as this all was happening, I could not believe it. The lady who'd sat next to me at lunch made it across after me, very audibly upset.

Once the last person made it through the last river crossing, we cheered ecstatically.

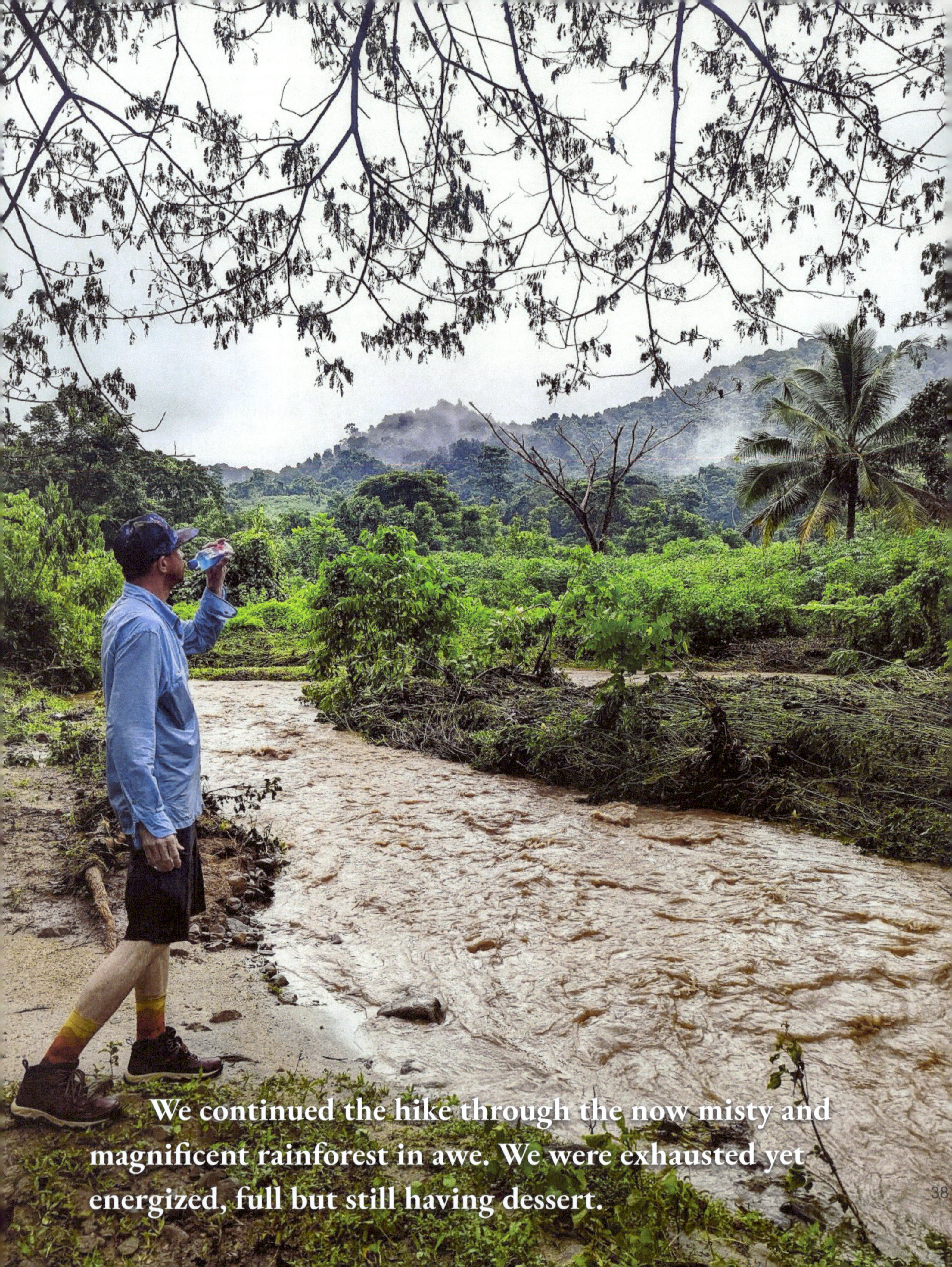

We continued the hike through the now misty and magnificent rainforest in awe. We were exhausted yet energized, full but still having dessert.

Before getting on the bus, I thanked the guys for saving our lives. Although my underwear and towel were now thoroughly soaked in Damon's pockets, I was grateful to have a dry change of clothes on the bus. I asked everyone on the bus whether, after all that, anyone lost anything. Everyone shook their heads no, impressed.

Just before taking off, a villager handed something to Grace.

"Hey, whose shirt is this?" she asked, holding it up as it dripped into the pool forming on the bus floor. It was mine; I realized I must have set it down outside while changing. The shirt was still white.

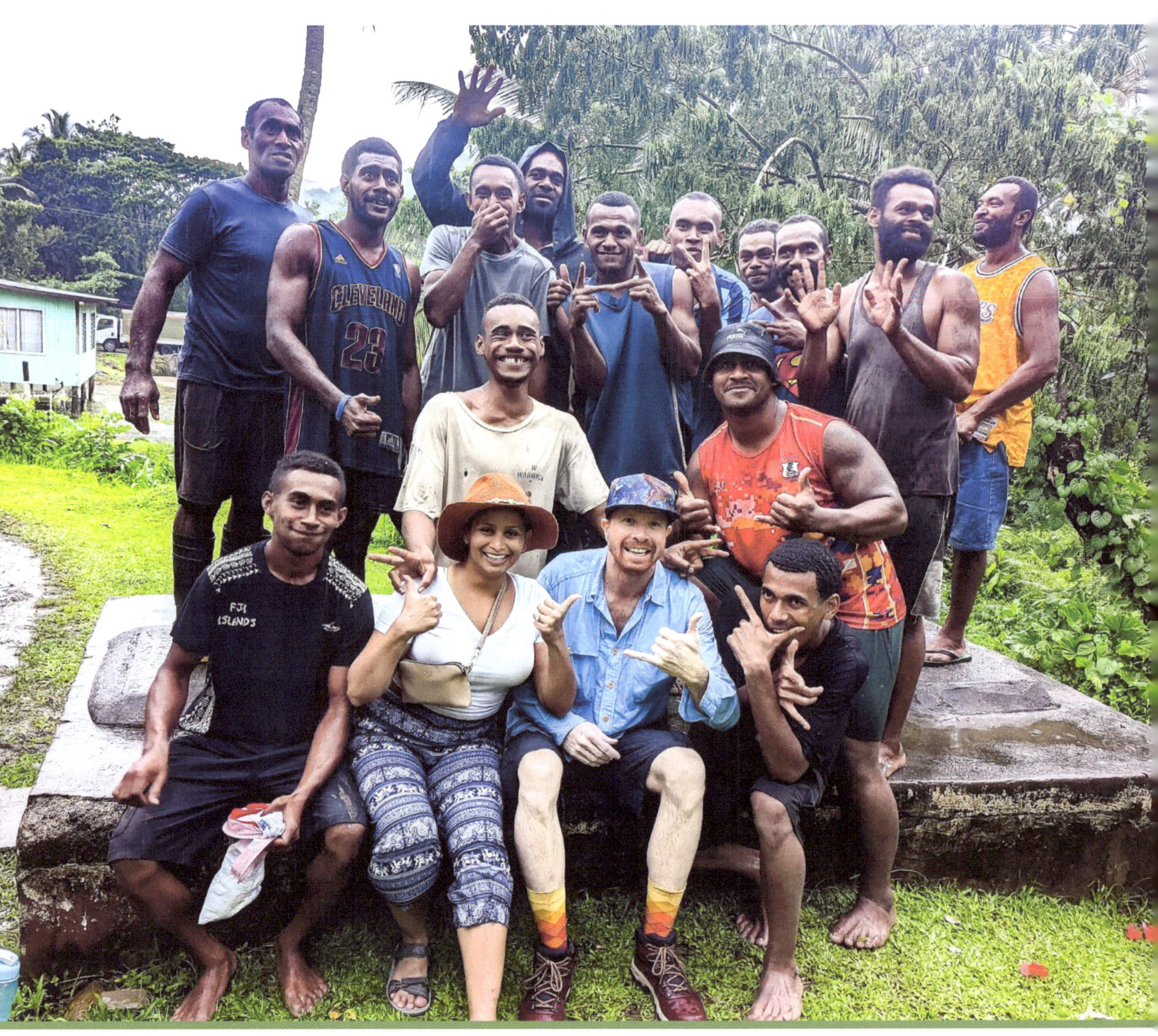